I'm Reading About

NEBRASKA

The Cornhusker State!

I0888721

GALLOPADE

by Carole Marsh

Printed and Manufactured in Peachtree City, GA., USA
www.gallopade.com

Book design: John Hanson

Editorial manager: Janice Baker

Current Edition ©2017

Nebraska is a great state.
It is one of a kind.

What makes Nebraska special?
Let's read about it
and see!

NATIVE AMERICANS

Who lived in Nebraska first?

Native Americans did!

They moved around to find food.
They hunted for animals to eat.
They fished in Nebraska's rivers.
They gathered fruits and seeds and nuts.

EXPLORERS

Meriwether Lewis and William Clark
came to Nebraska in 1804.
They were traveling along the Missouri River.
President Thomas Jefferson sent them
to explore new territory!

Lewis and Clark learned about
Nebraska's plants and animals.
They wrote about what they saw in their journals.

HISTORY

Many Americans moved west to start new lives in Nebraska.
They traveled to Nebraska in covered wagons.
They built houses out of prairie grass and sod.

Settlers on the Great Plains built sod houses because there were few trees for log cabins!

Nebraska Prairie Home

STATEHOOD

Nebraska was the 37th state
to join the United States of America!

Isn't it great,
to be a state!
I bet Nebraska
could hardly wait!

Nebraska became a state in 1867.

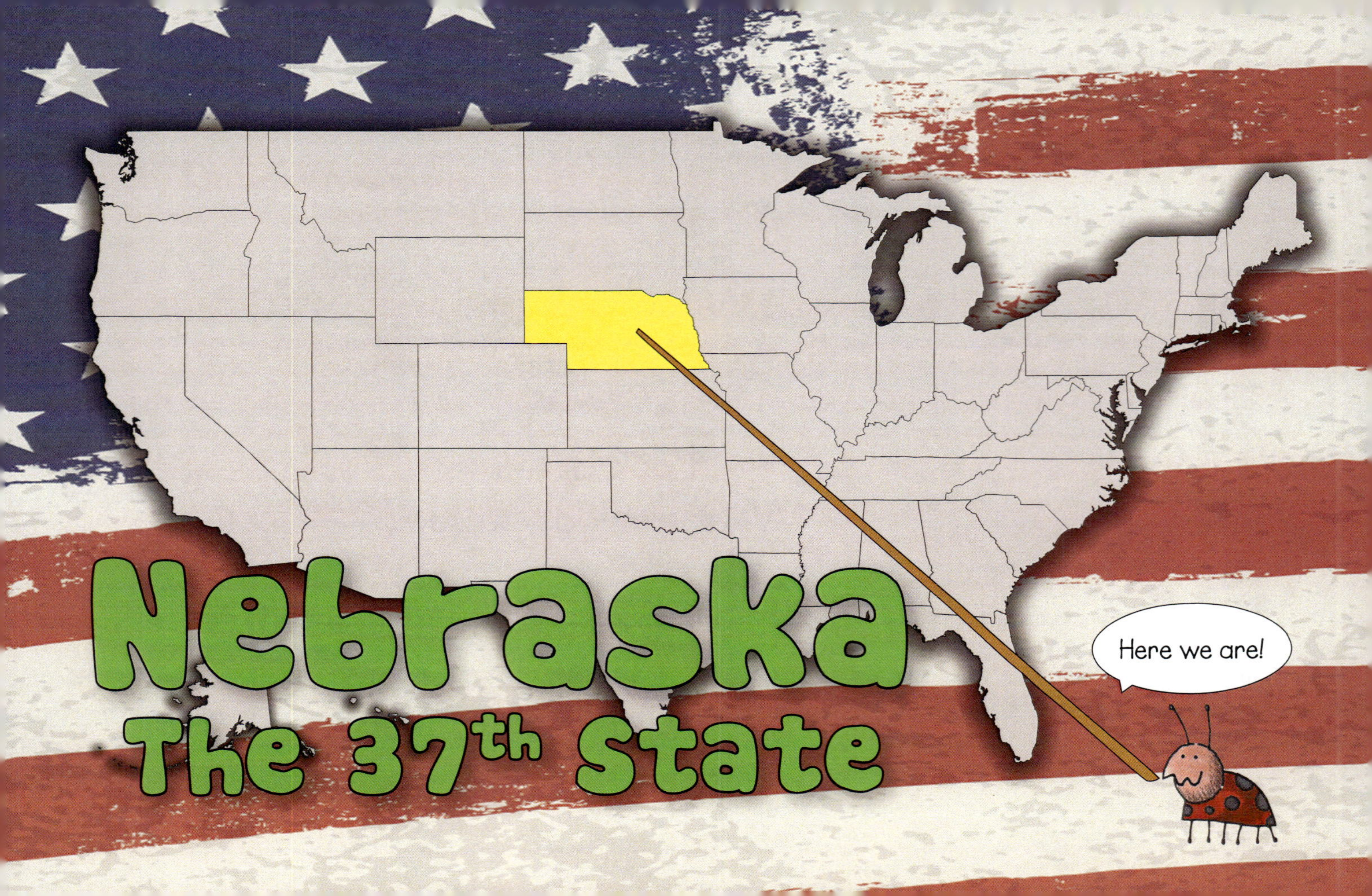
Nebraska
The 37th State
Here we are!

FLAG

I am the state flag.
I was adopted in 1925.

What color am I?
I am blue.

Look at me.
What else do you see?

I fly high over the state of Nebraska!

GREAT SEAL OF THE STATE OF NEBRASKA
EQUALITY BEFORE THE LAW
MARCH 1ST 1867

CAPITAL

Say hello to Lincoln,
the capital city of Nebraska!

There is an important building in Lincoln.
It is the State Capitol.
Nebraska's laws are made there!

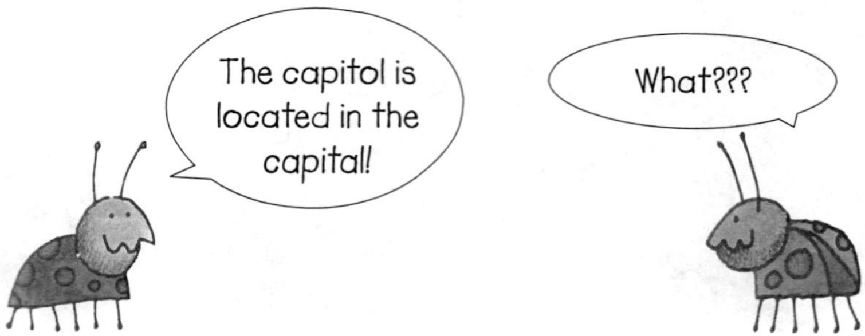

Lincoln
Lincoln
Capital

SEAL

I am a seal,
but I am not the State Seal.
If I were, I would be very important.
I would be stamped on many official papers.
(Ouch, that might hurt!)

GREAT SEAL OF THE STATE OF NEBRASKA
EQUALITY BEFORE THE LAW
MARCH 1ST 1867

Now, that's official!

NICKNAME

State nicknames are fun!
State nicknames are great!
They share fun facts
about each state!

Nebraska's nickname is "The Cornhusker State."

Nebraska, Iowa, and Illinois produce almost half of the nation's grain corn!

The Cornhusker State

BORDERS

Look at Nebraska.
Nebraska is in a region called "the Midwest."

Nebraska borders six other states.
Find them on the map!

Borders

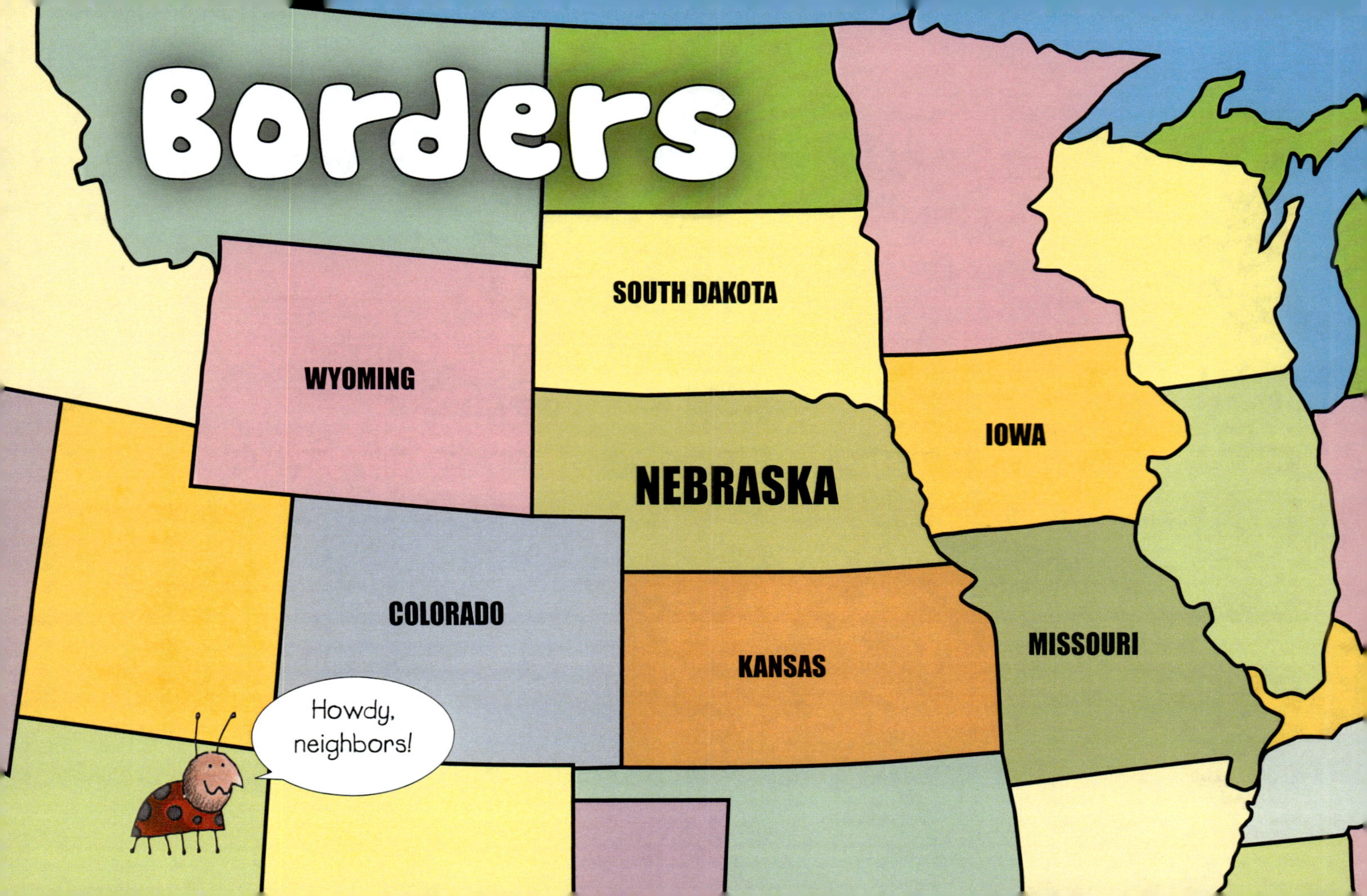
SOUTH DAKOTA
WYOMING
IOWA
NEBRASKA
COLORADO
MISSOURI
KANSAS
Howdy, neighbors!

PRESIDENT

Gerald Ford was the 38th President
of the United States of America.
He was born in Nebraska!

Gerald Ford was born in Omaha.
Gerald was a Boy Scout.
He attained the highest rank in Boy Scouts.
He became an Eagle Scout!

Gerald Ford

PEOPLE

Many famous people

Red Cloud

Warrior and Oglala Lakota Chief

Susan LaFlesche Picotte

First Native American woman to earn a medical degree

Willa Cather

Author who wrote about life on the Great Plains

call our state home!

William "Buffalo Bill" Cody

U.S. Army scout, buffalo hunter, and entertainer

Fred Astaire

Dancer on Broadway and in Hollywood films

Andy Roddick

World-champion professional tennis player

Western Meadowlark

I am the state bird, and I fly
over Nebraska, proud and high.

As I fly, up in the sky,
I flap my wings to tell you "Hi!"

The Nebraska state bird is the Western Meadowlark.

BIRD

Goldenrod

FLOWER

I am the Goldenrod.
I am the state flower.

I grow where it's warm and sunny.
I bloom in summer and fall.
I help make Nebraska beautiful!

Look at me! Smell me!
My blossoms are bright yellow!

Cottonwood
That's a big tree!

TREE

I am a Cottonwood—I'm the state tree.
All over Nebraska is where to find me.

My roots run deep, they keep me strong.
I can live hundreds of years—that's very long!

I stand up straight, big and tall.
Don't climb too high—it would hurt to fall!

Honeybee

INSECT

I am the Honeybee.
I am the state insect.

I might sting you if you bother me.
But really, I am your friend.

I carry pollen from flower to flower.
I make honey.
I help Nebraska crops grow.

BZZZZZZZZZZZZ!

Prairies

PRAIRIES

Let's go to the prairie!

Nebraska has miles of prairies.
The tall golden grass
sways in the breeze.

The prairie is flat,
There are no trees.
It stretches as far as the eye can see!

Nebraska's prairies are home to many animals:

Red-Tailed Hawks **Prairie Dogs** **Badgers** **Coyotes** **Bison** **and More!**

Rivers

RIVERS

Nebraska's rivers are the place to be.
Fishing, boating, swimming—
fun for you and me.

Rivers wind across the state.
Settlers used them to move
crops, animals, and freight!

Loess Hills

LOESS HILLS

There are hills in eastern Nebraska.
They are called the "Loess Hills."
Loose soil blown by the wind formed these hills.
It took many, many years to do it.

This habitat is home to many animals:

Deer Foxes Turtles Birds Butterflies and More!

Loess comes from a German word that means "loose."

Chimney Rock

Chimney Rock is a tall rock!
It looks like a chimney towering above the prairie.
Pioneers used Chimney Rock as a landmark
on the Oregon Trail.
They wrote about Chimney Rock in their journals!

Chimney Rock is made of clay
and sandstone.
Some pioneers climbed up and
carved their names into it!

LANDMARK

Nebraska Crops

AGRICULTURE

Nebraska has many farms.
Why?
Because Nebraska has good soil and a mild climate!

Some of the top crops grown in Nebraska are:

Corn **Soybeans** **Wheat** **Sorghum**

Sports in Nebraska

Baseball! Basketball! Football!
Nebraska has it all.

Whether you like to watch or play,
You are sure to have a ball!

Cornhuskers **Mavericks**

Bluejays

& More!

Nebraska: Home of Kool-Aid

CLAIM TO FAME

Kool-Aid was invented in Hastings, Nebraska!
Edwin Perkins created the drink in 1927.
The first six flavors were:

strawberry **lemon-lime** **raspberry**

cherry **grape** **orange**

Kool-Aid is the official soft drink of the state of Nebraska!

GLOSSARY

attain: succeed in achieving something

climate: weather conditions in an area over a long period of time

freight: goods transported by truck, train, ship, or aircraft

habitat: a place where plants or animals naturally live

journal: a personal record of news and events

laws: rules made by the government

pollen: a yellow powder that helps plants make new plants

region: an area that has similar characteristics

sod: a section of grass–covered soil held together by roots

sorghum: a grain often used for animal feed